Presented To:

_____

From:

_____

Date:

_____

Baby's First Book of Blessings

BY MELODY CARLSON
ILLUSTRATED BY JUDITH PFEIFFER

ZONDERkidz

ZONDERKIDZ

Baby's First Book of Blessings
Copyright © 2005 by Melody Carlson
Illustrations © 2005 by Judith Pfeiffer

Zonderkidz, 3950 Sparks Drive SE, Suite 101, Grand Rapids, Michigan 49546

Published in Grand Rapids, Michigan, by Zonderkidz. Zonderkidz is a
registered trademark of The Zondervan Corporation, L.L.C., a wholly owned
subsidiary of HarperCollins Christian Publishing, Inc.

Requests for information should be addressed to
customercare@harpercollins.com.

Hardcover ISBN 978-0-310-73077-4
Ebook ISBN 978-0-310-73079-8

Art Direction: Laura M. Maitner
Cover Design Update: Diane Mielke

Printed in Penang, Malaysia

24 25 26 27 28 /SEM/ 10 9 8 7 6 5 4 3 2

For my sweet little granddaughter,
Anika Margaret Carlson (born 7/1/04)
With love always, Nana.

~M.C.

To Babies Everywhere
Peace 🌸 Love ❤
Health 🍎 & Smiles 🐻

~J.P.

Contents

1

Count My Blessings

I count my blessings

Every day,

When I rest

And when I play.

2

My Big Breakfast

Bacon, eggs, and toast

Are yummy.

God blesses me

And fills my tummy.

3

My Two Eyes

I count my eyes,

One and two.

God blesses me

When I see you!

4

Ears to Hear

Songs and stories

Are mine to hear.

God blessed me with

Two listening ears.

5

Feet That Go

I jump and skip and

Hop for fun.

God blessed me with

Two feet that run.

6

Comfy Laps

Warm and snuggly,

Great for naps.

God blesses me

With comfy laps.

7

My Mommy's Here

When I need her

She is there.

God blesses me

With Mommy's care.

8

My Daddy's Home!

When he comes home,

I am so glad!

God blessed me with

My great big dad.

9

My Happy Family

Mommy and Daddy

And me—that's three!

God blessed me with

My family.

10

Grandpa and Me

Hand in hand,

We take fun walks.

God blesses me

When Grandpa talks.

11

Grandma's Hugs

She loves me so

And gives warm snugs.

God blesses me

With Grandma's hugs.

12

'Round My Table

At dinnertime

I take my place.

God blesses me

When Dad says grace.

13

My Cozy Coat

When I go out

I wear my hood.

God blessed me with

A coat that's good.

14

Riding in the Car

Snug in my carseat,

I wave and smile.

God blesses me

With every mile.

15

At the Store

Our cart is filled

With food galore!

God blessed me at

The grocery store.

16

My Front Porch

I sit and dream and

Sometimes sing.

God blesses me

On our porch swing.

17

I Can Help

I rake the leaves up

By myself.

God blesses me

With hands that help.

18

Fun with Friends

Jane and Sam have

Come to play.

God blessed me with

Two friends today.

19

Neighbor Friends

The folks next door

Are kind and good.

God blessed me with

Our neighborhood.

20

My Bear Friend

My bear is great for

Cozy snuggles.

God blesses me

With fuzzy huggles.

21

Counting Fish

One, two, three—

Their tails go swish.

God blesses me

With my goldfish.

22

My Furry Friends

I have three kitties—

Hear them purr.

God blesses me

With friends in fur.

23

Singing Birds

Robins and sparrows

On the wing.

God blesses me

With birds that sing.

24

At the Zoo

Zebras, bears, and

Monkeys too.

God blesses me

While at the zoo.

25

Wading Pool Fun

One, two, three

Kids in my pool.

God blesses me

While we stay cool.

26

Goofy Giggles

I laugh and shriek

If someone tickles.

God blesses me

With goofy giggles.

27

Sailing Boats

One, two, three—

Watch them float.

God blesses me

With my toy boats.

28

Playing in the Park

Swings and slides and

Merry-go-rounds.

God blesses me

With this playground.

29

Making Merry Music

Horns and drums and

Music toys.

God blesses me

With happy noise.

30

Time to Rest

I get cranky

Not my best.

God blesses me

With a short rest.

31

Sunny Sunshine

I feel warm sunshine

On my face.

God blesses me

In this bright place!

32

My Garden Grows

Corn, peas, carrots

In a row.

God blesses me

With things that grow.

33

Tall, Tall Trees

I see tall branches

Touch the sky.

God blesses me

With trees so high.

34

Snowy Days

My two mittens

Make a ball.

God blesses me

With fresh snowfall.

35

Making Mud Pies

After rain has washed

The skies,

God blesses me

With big mud pies!

36

Bathtub Bubbles

Toys and bubbles

Help me scrub.

God blesses me

With my bathtub.

37

My Toothbrush

I clean each tooth,

I don't rush.

God blesses me

with my toothbrush.

38

My Storybook

We snuggle close

To take a look.

God blessed me with

My storybook.

39

My Bedtime Prayer

I thank God for his

Love and care.

God blesses me

With bedtime prayer.

40

Sweet Moonlight

The sky is dark

And it is night.

God blesses me

With sweet moonlight.

41

Counting My Blessings

I count my blessings

Just like sheep.

God blesses me

And helps me sleep.

Amen.